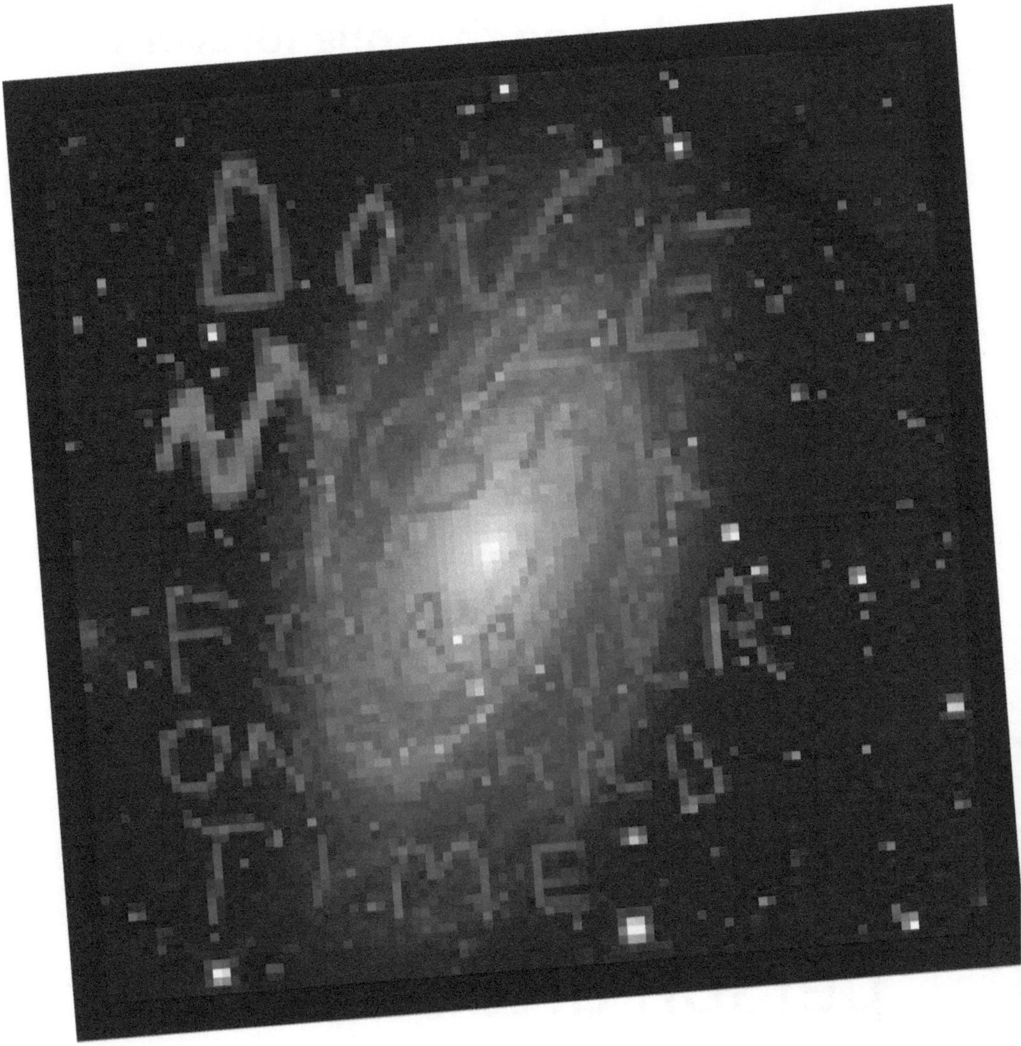

The story behind the song forever on thru time and other songs released on Itunes by singer songwriter Dove Night*

Hello ! from Dove

this is a romantic song! it is about falling in love with the right person after many years of being alone ! it is an up-tempo pop rock to mellow rock song! I hope you like it ,now here are the lyrics

instrumental intro

I spent so many years feeling alone and sad

its because I never
had been loved
because I thought I was
bad

   pre chorus- then you
came into my life and I
am so amazed because
you 're all mine
   forever on thru time

chorus - so I 'm happy to be ,by your side

because we 'll stay together forever on thru time

and when you're not around ,I still feel loved

because at the end of the day, you 're always at home

instrumental intro

There was a time when I felt I was dying

In the past, all through my life ,there was no one besides me

pre chorus

chorus

guitar solo /

instrumental solo

prechorus \\

chorus

instrumental

interlude -

forever!!!!!!!!!!!!!!!!!!

Forever on thru time ,
the beginnings

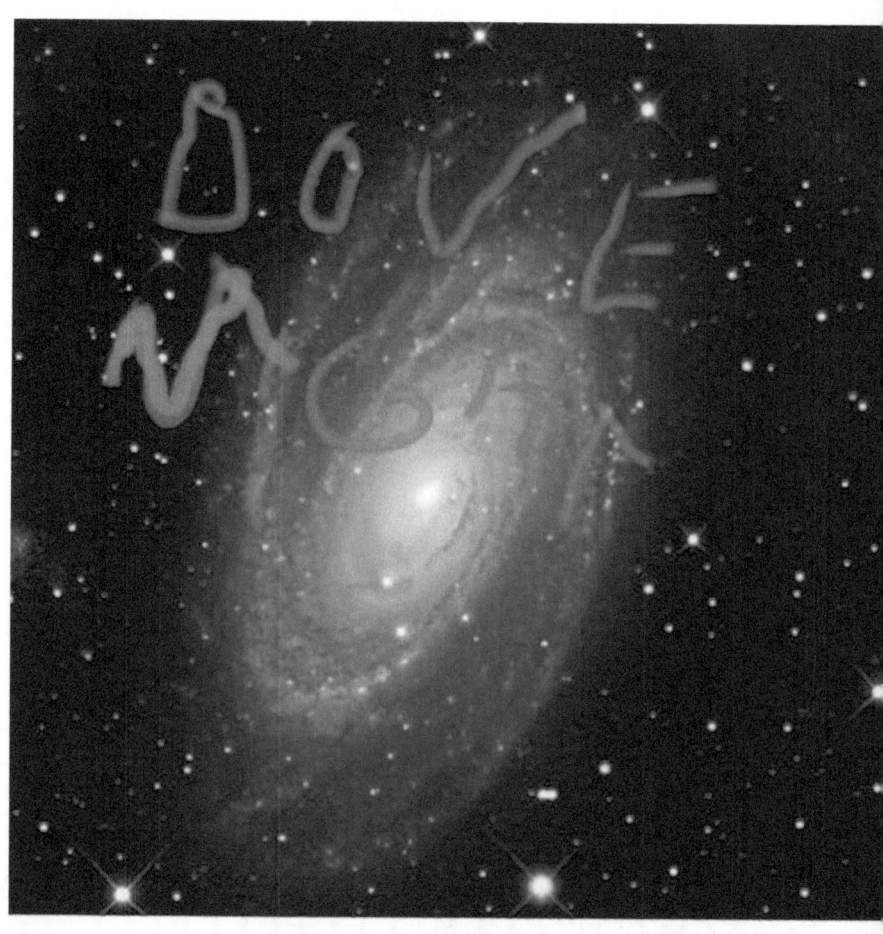

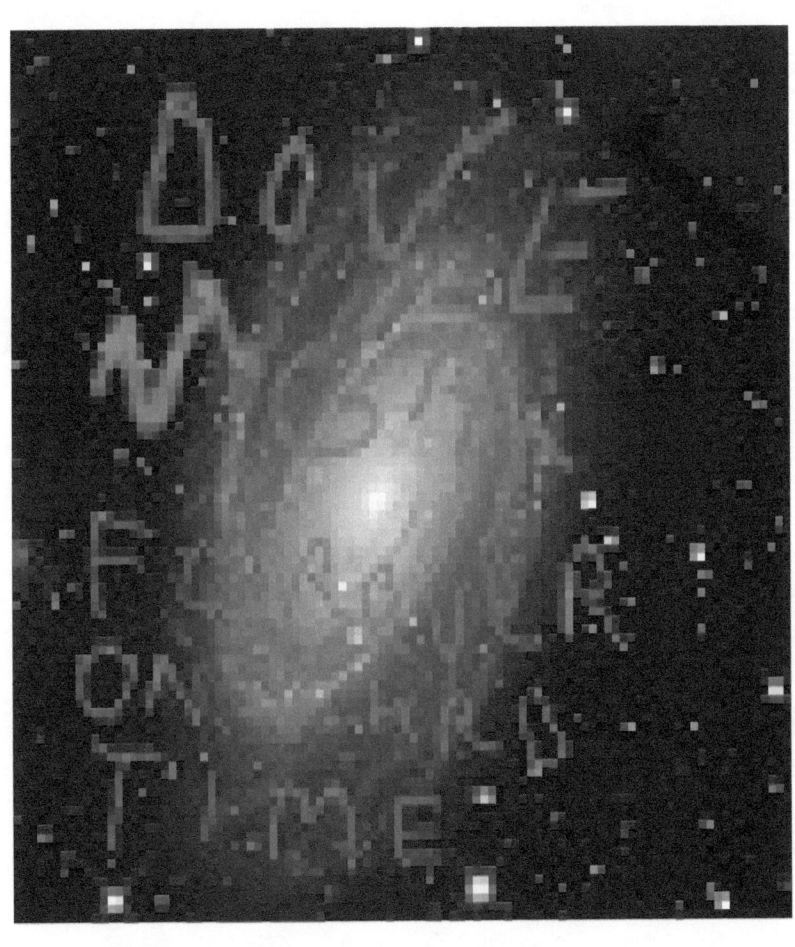

Forever on thru time is a song about finding true love after many years of not finding the right person or being alone. I am one person who spent many years being alone so the song is definitely biographical but many people can relate to being alone or spending many years with the wrong person. Sometimes love takes time and sometimes it can take years.

This picture below is the symbol of the song forever on thru time as well as for myself .When You think of dove night ,think of the blue space atmosphere which is symbol of my cool , nice personality who is also anunique person that belongs in space. Please you guys out there, Please take me there. I perform clubs for several years.Ipaid my dues but it up to karma and karma and God states that I must perform somehow.But overall, I leave my life, my destiny up to GOD and that is all I am going to do.

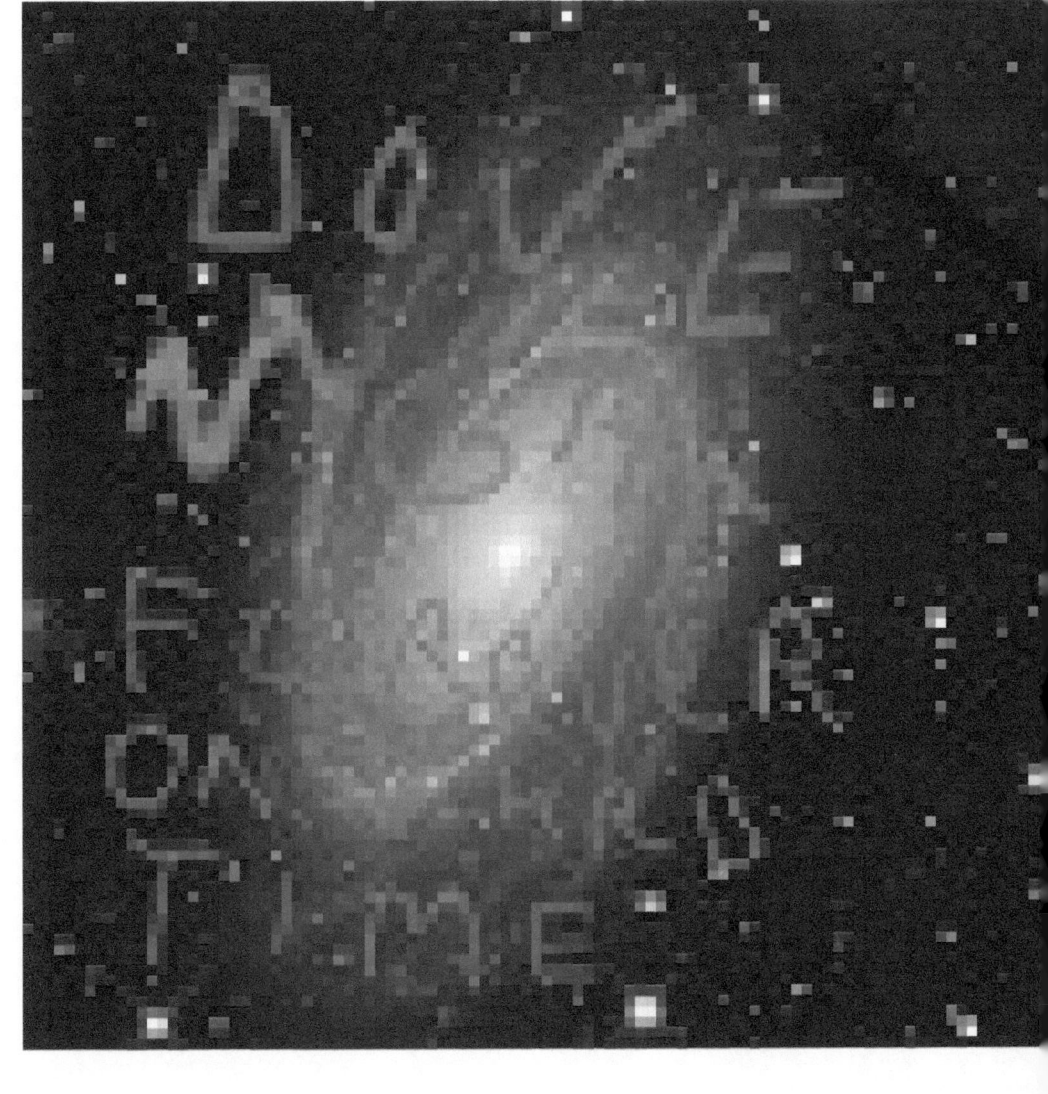

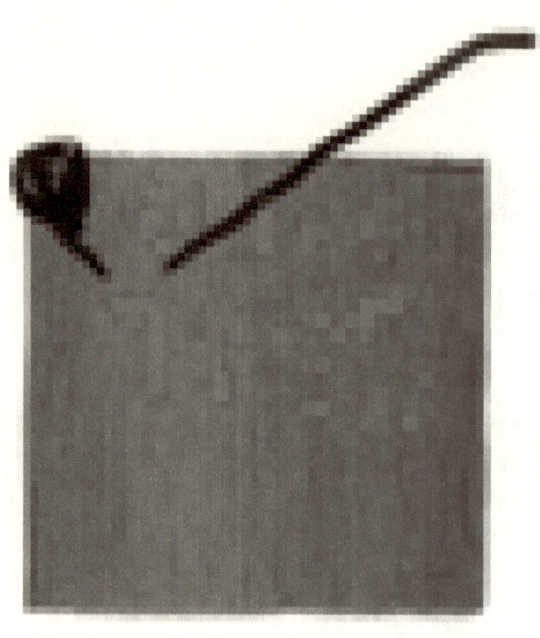

The song Unique

The song Unique is about my nice off beat personality and look and how it has been marginalized by prejudiced people who want a singer who looks like these singers below.

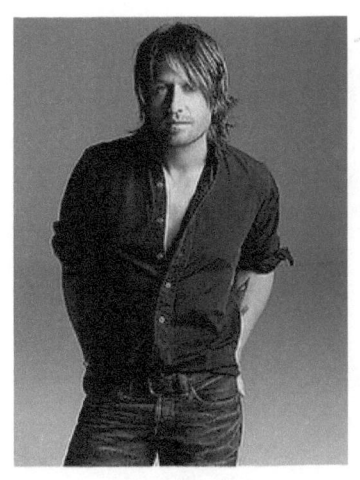
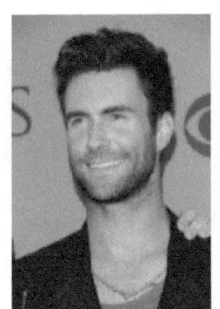

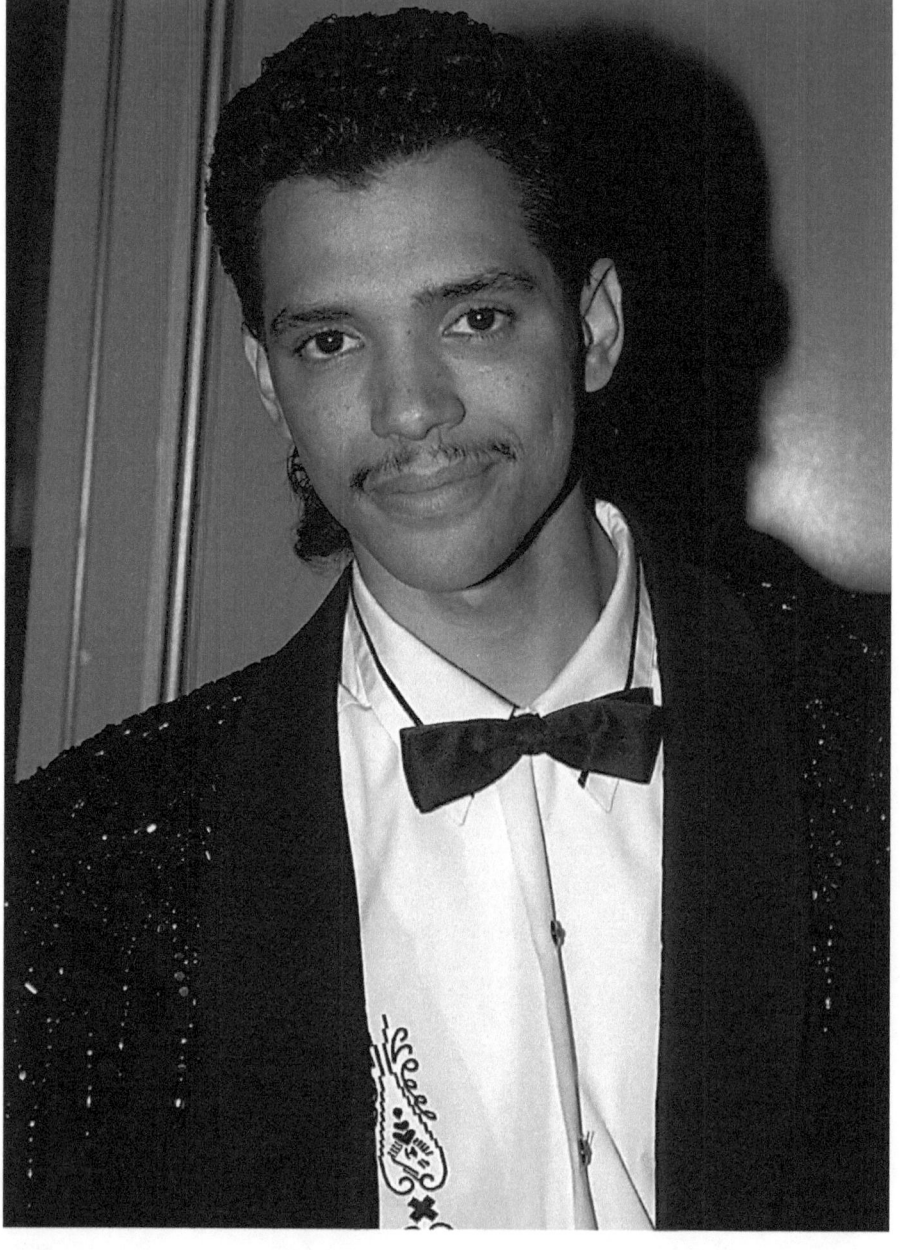

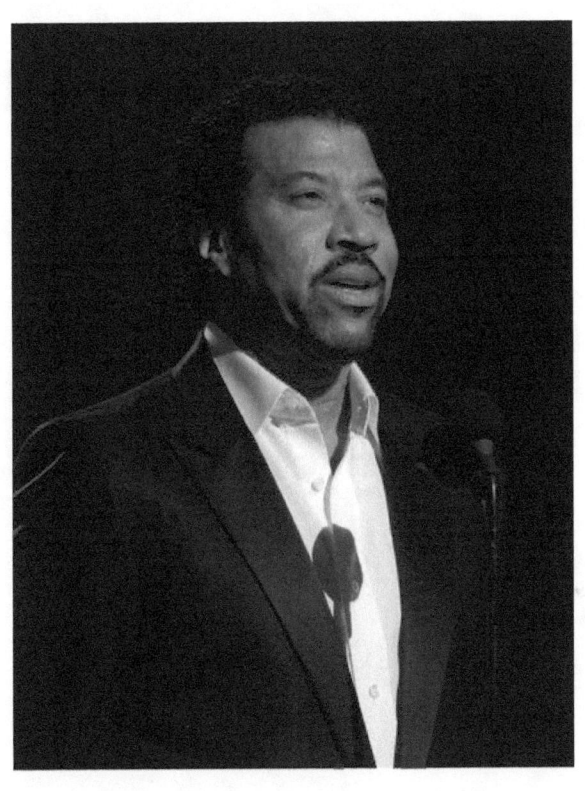

Because of this
shallowness and my
size. I was told by an AR

person that I could not
be famous so that is
the inspiration for me
in writing the song
"Unique.

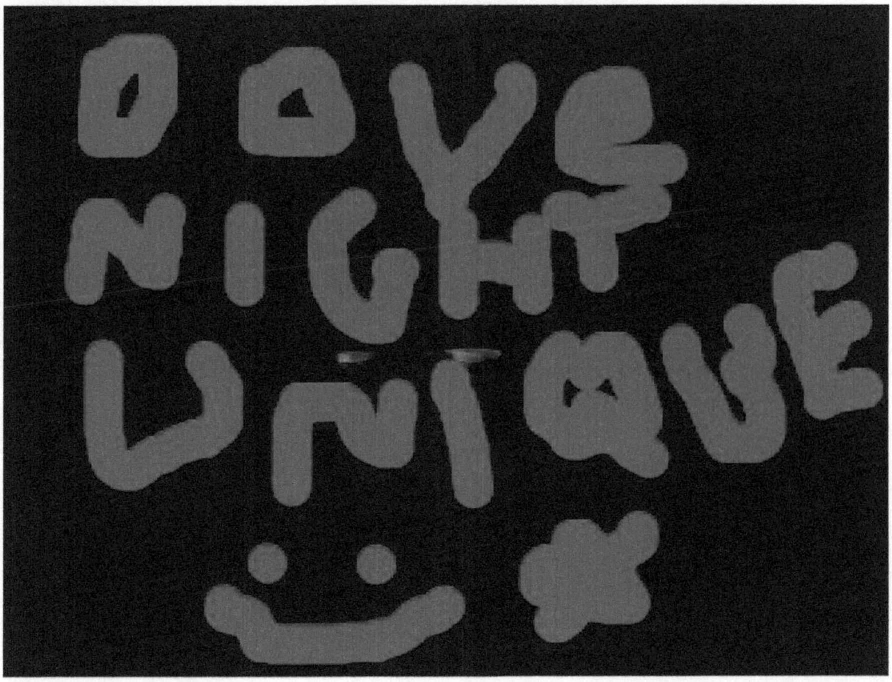
DDYS
NIGHT
UNIQUE

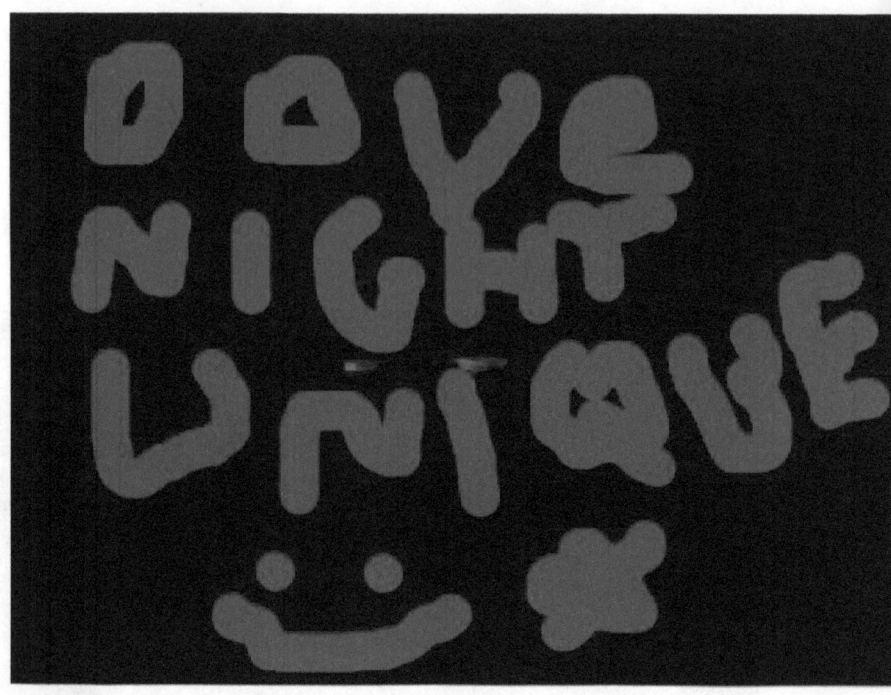

DOVES RECORDS is owned by CD baby, not me. But you can look up the song on itunes

If you could really see me, I would look like an intellectual type yet I am an unique individual and I like to be that way.   Dove Night

I am a very tall big guy who loves to sing and have fun . I truly apologize to those who wants only the stereotype performer / artist

Dove night

I am a good songwriter, I can sound like mick jagger and bon jovi (guys who are very talented musically.I love to make up melodies ,so if someone wanted to use my songs for others. I would let them . Dove night

When I was younger I was influenced strongly by the guy below ,a completely different person than me.

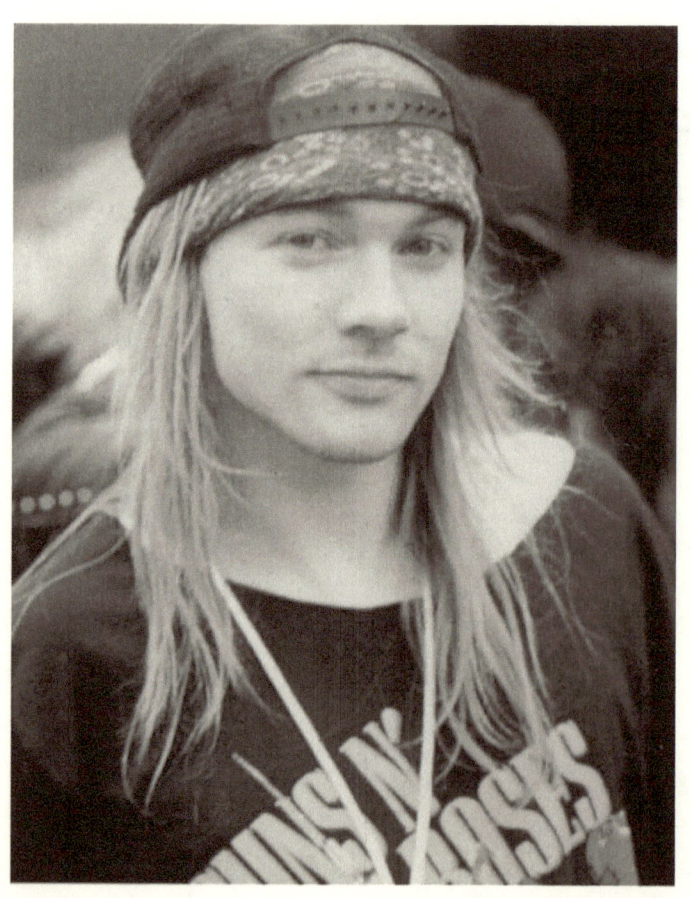

The reasons were because I thought Axl was unique, Very Unique and his off beat style was influential despite whatever controversies there were in the late 80's .I was heavily influenced by Freddie mercury, Michael Jackson and Led Zeppelin, beatles, Jimi Hendrix and Bon Jovi for his methodical approach to music . Another band I admired for their audacity for wear makeup below .

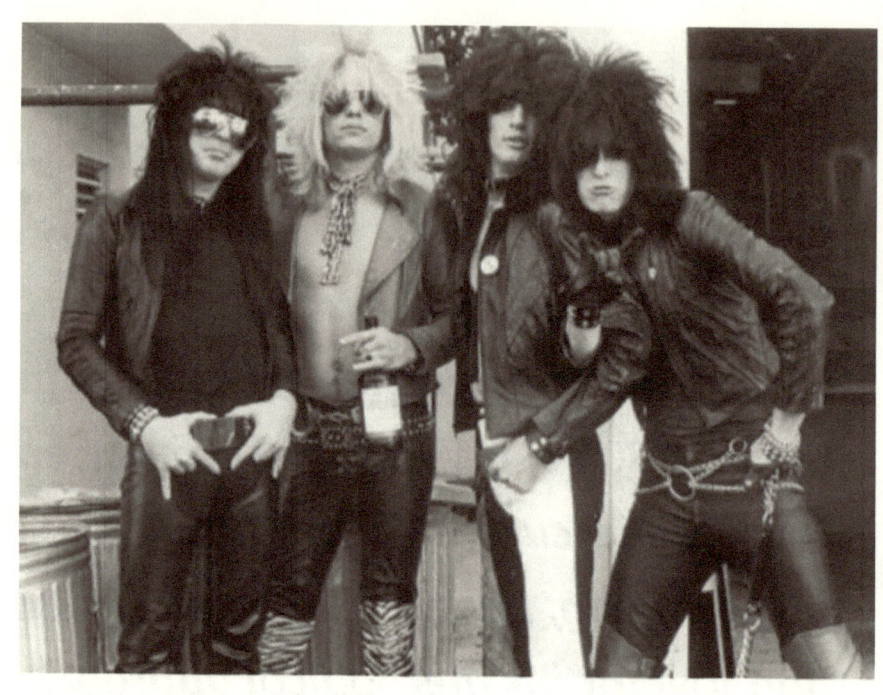

BUT THE ONE WHO REALLY INFLUENCED ME A LOT WERE NIRVANA <AND PEARL JAM BECAUSE OF THEIR songs about depression, teen angst and liberalism beliefs,**SEATTLE IS WHERE I BELONG >** I can relate to them a lot *because I had a very bad childhood SO JEREMY SPOKE IN CLASS TODAY I CAN RELATE TO AS WELL AS LITHIUM AND Rape me.*

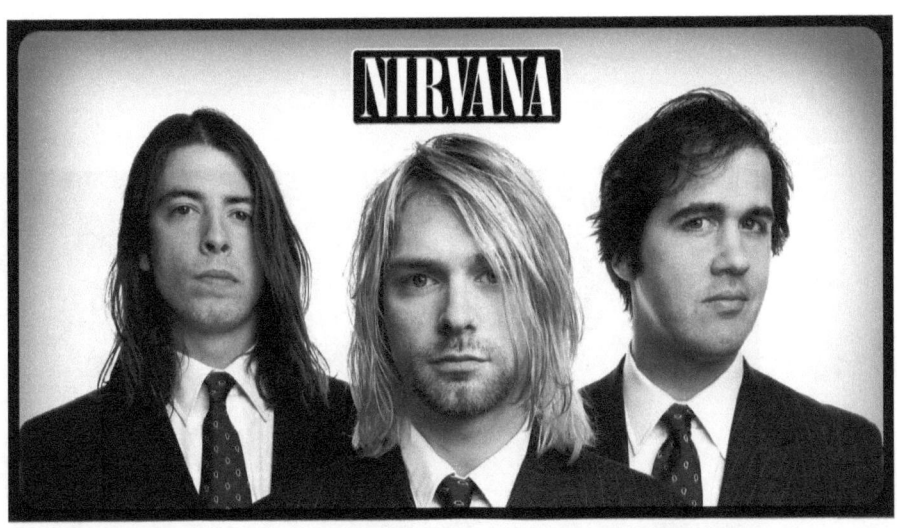

Pearl jam

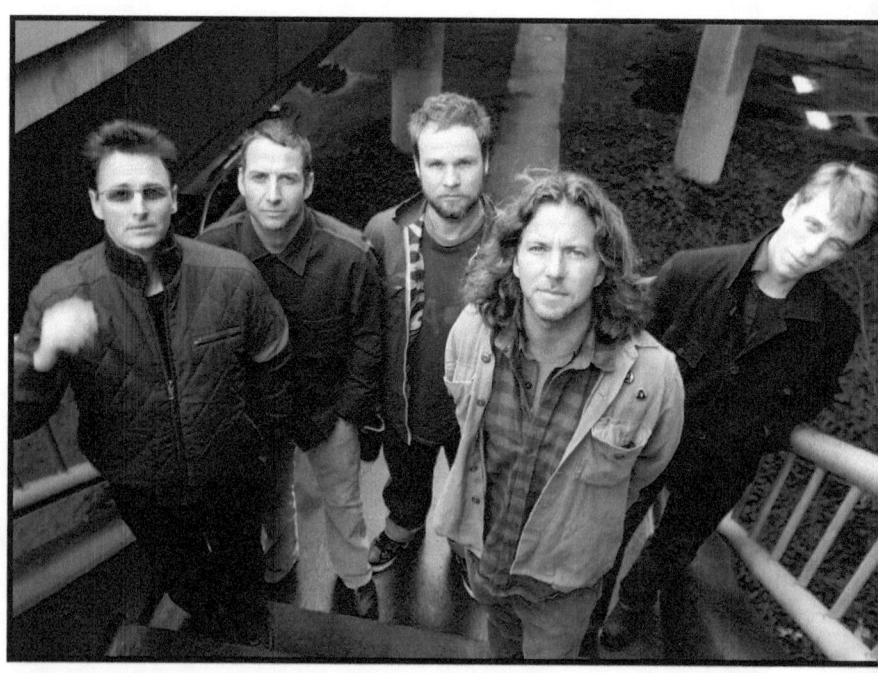

Oh course I like soul , country ,
classical ,you name it . In soul ,there is
Aretha franklin and Michael Jackson but
Michael Jackson is pop music so he

does not count . the guy here is not soul but rock n roll

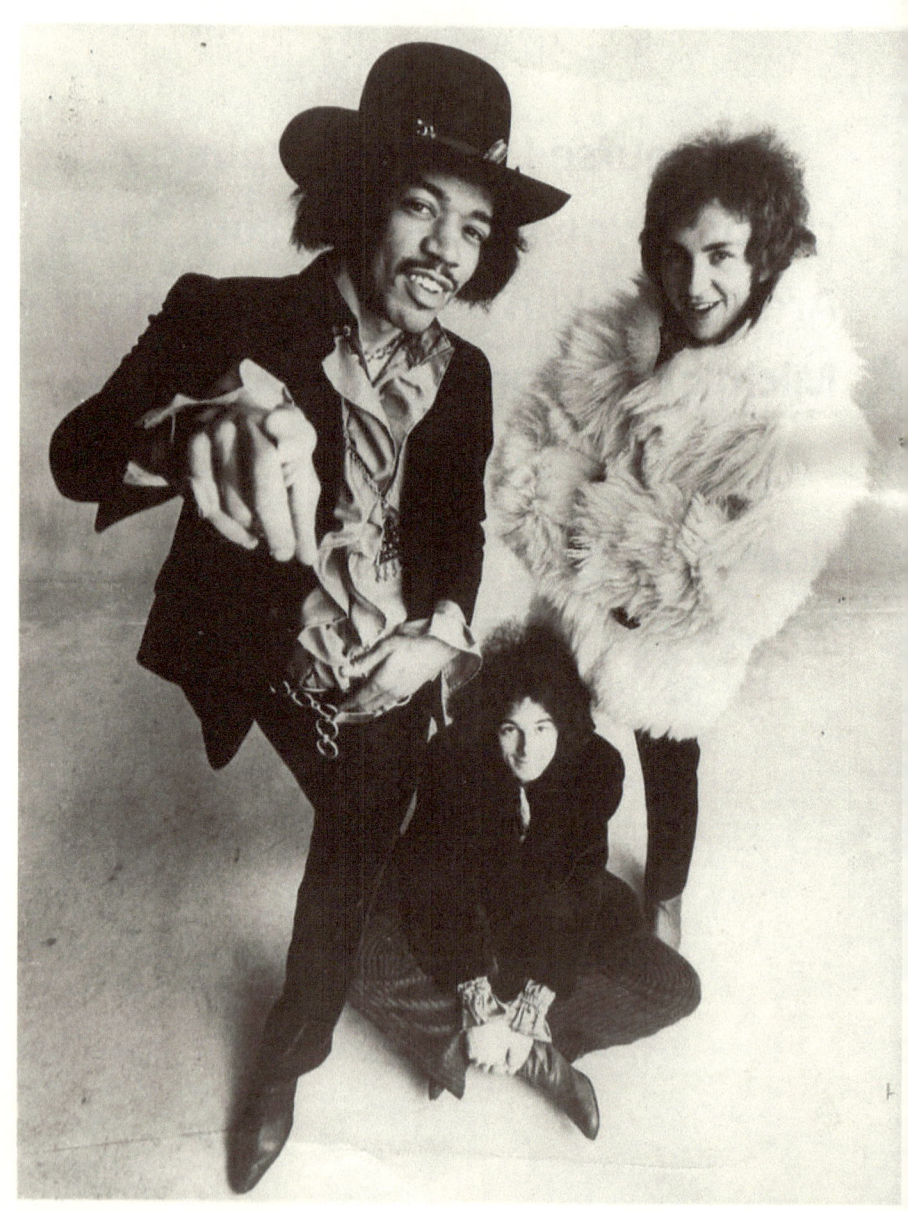

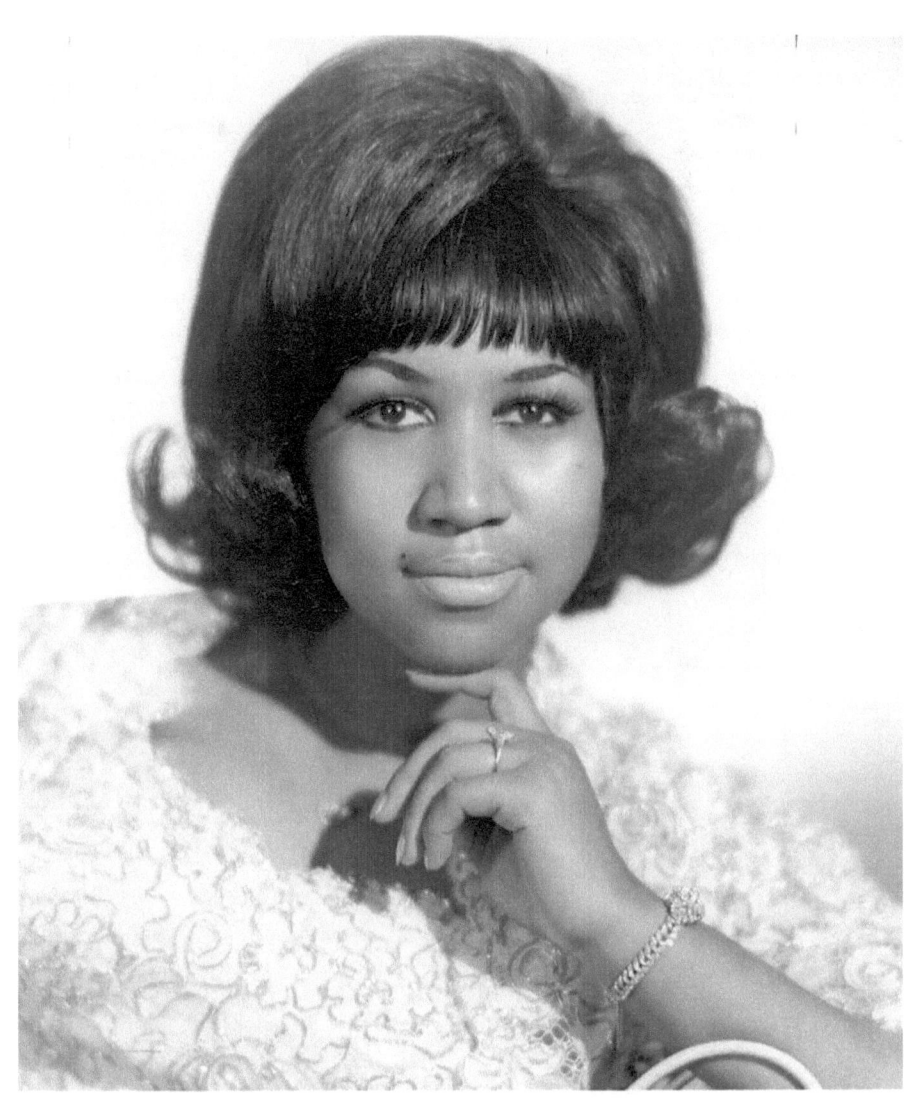

https://www.google.com/url?sa=t&rct=j&q=&esrc=s&source=web&cd=1&cad=rja&uact=8&sqi=2&ved=0CLoBEN8sMABqFQoTCOmWtJzIusgCFRfTYwodGroHsA&url=http%3A%2F%2Fen.musicplayon.com%2Fplay%3Fv%3D359715&usg=AFQjCNF_JDOvnJ37QYWlB-OT7Z6QpcmmHg&bvm=bv.104819420,d.cGc

I like garth brooks, Faiith hill,some of reba mcentire, and willie nelson

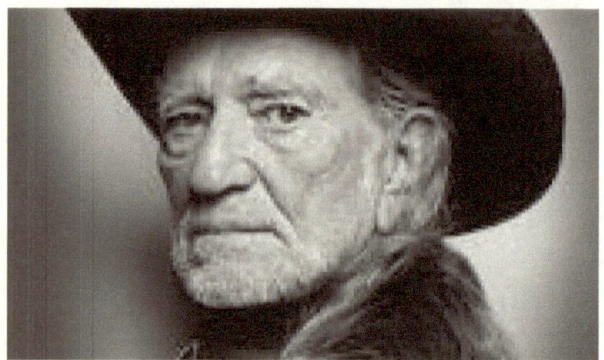

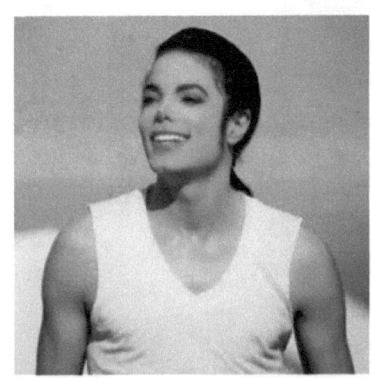

pop

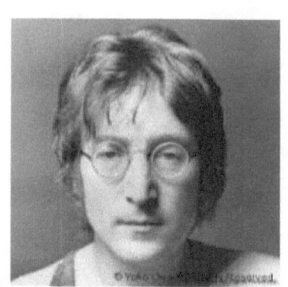

And rock

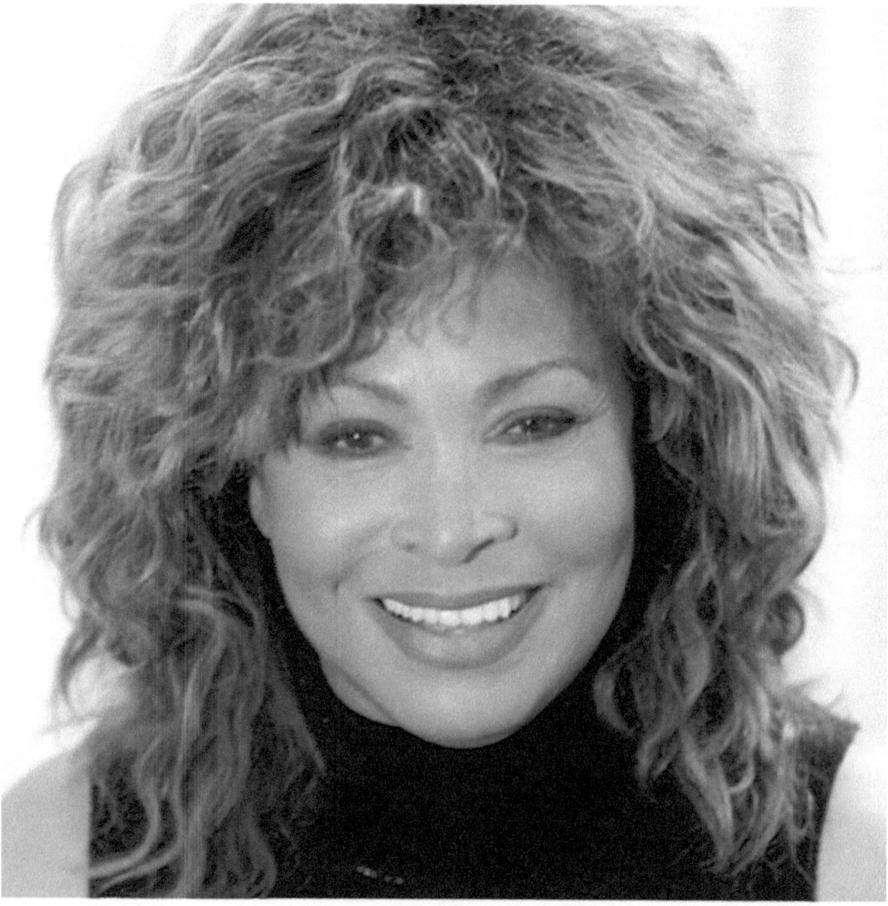

And Mozart

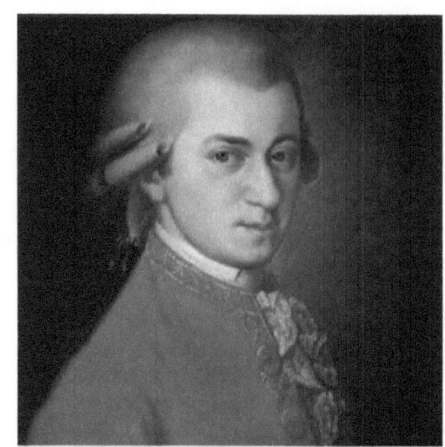

country

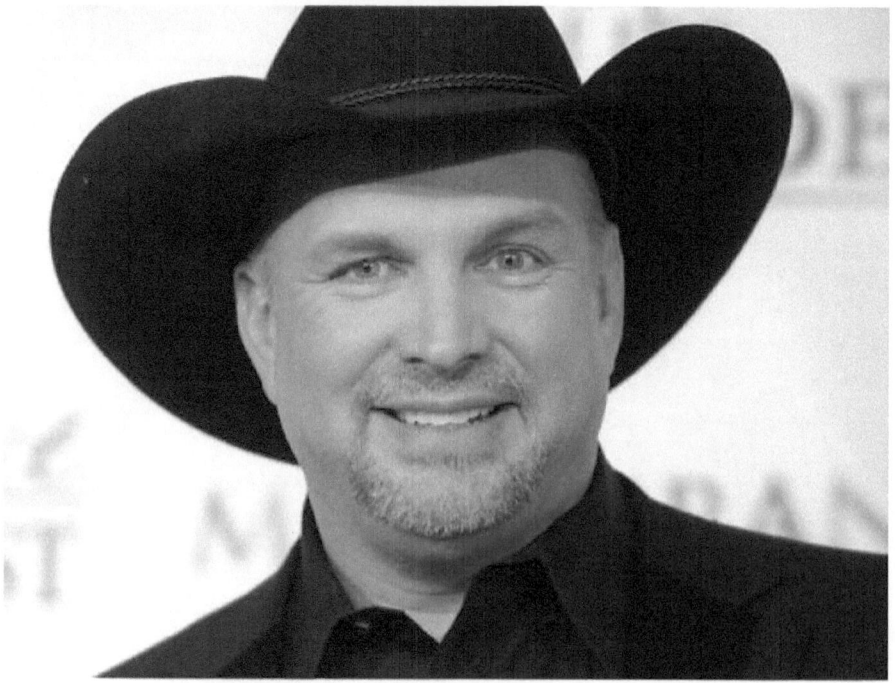

I L ike elvis and some of prince too

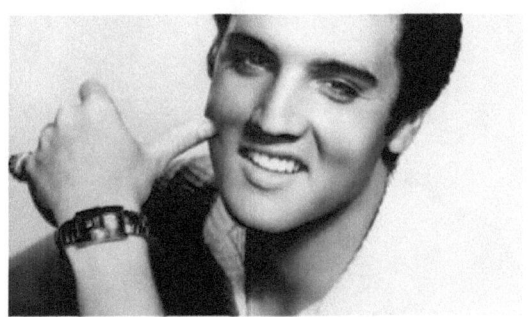

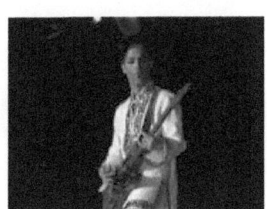

You want to get my songs and ron misrach contact doves records /cd baby and

ituneshttps://itunes.apple.com/gb/album/forever-on-thru-time-single/id688630290

https://itunes.apple.com/gb/album/unique-single/id882958642

https://itunes.apple.com/gb/music-video/forever-on-thru-time/id992438497

https://itunes.apple.com/us/album/ boyriend-in-a-drawer- single/id792817756

goodbye

www.ingramcontent.com/pod-product-compliance
Lightning Source LLC
Chambersburg PA
CBHW021939170526
45157CB00005B/2357